"… an invitation to eavesdrop on the creative process and whirring mind of a slam poet preacher who cares deeply about testing the faith of his audience without giving a fuck about their sensibilities." **Damien Becker**

"… reveals the slam poet's arsenal (with the emphasis on arse). **Sarah Temporal, performance poet and educator, sarahtemporal.com**

"… poking at every taboo with a curious balance of frivolity and utmost respect. I don't quite know how he does it, but the way he wears a privileged context with an almost crude boldness while still managing to be culturally sensitive is astounding. He is a provocative voice in the poetic and religious community, and a flavour that I'm very happy exists." **Hunter Wynn, performance poet**

Also by Jason John

Worshipping Evolution's God

A Walk in the Park

Easter Horror Stories

Coming Soon:

Christian Sex Today:
Advice from Moses, Paul, Jesus and Darwin

jasonjohn.com.au

I'm not a racist but...

I've got a racist butt.

Jason John

Copyright 2020, all rights reserved.

ISBN: (paperback)   978-0-6488257-0-8
ISBN: (ePub)   978-0-6488257-1-5

The right of Jason John to be identified as the author of this book has been asserted by him in accordance with the *Copyright Amendment (Moral Rights) Act 2000.*

This work is copyright as spelt out in the Australian Copyright Act 1968.

In addition, up to ten lines of any one poem may be reproduced in any form, with explicit acknowledgment of this work, provided that no monies are generated by such reproduction. In other words, don't pinch a cool line and print it on a t-shirt for profit.

One single poem may be used for educational purposes without permission, but with acknowledgment, provided that no monies are generated by such reproduction.

All other use requires the prior written permission of Jason John, via jasonrobertjohn@gmail.com

Cover photo: Jason John by Megan Carew (2019)
Rear Photo: Boggle eyes by Bruce Jacups (2019)

Thoughts on *I'm not a Racist, but*

"I'm Not A Racist But" is nothing you'd expect to read from a church minister but everything you've ever wanted one to say. Addressing politics, sex and religion with thought-provoking humour, this unorthodox collection makes no apologies for its audacious, controversial and challenging poems. Be prepared for your religious stereotypes to be smashed wide open in the most refreshing of ways. Jason is, without a doubt, the Australian Pete Holmes." - **Kathy Parker, writer, poet, author.**

"In these weird times, we need thinkers and communicators like Jason, more than ever." - **Jen.**

"The NSW Slam Poetry final was good. But Jason was really good." - **Emma.**

"Witty, inspirational, even educational. Jason delves into those parts of the shared human experience that are so often hidden and taboo… He goes straight to the heart of it, bursting it open, and dissecting it one bloody piece at a time. He's a truth teller, a stater of the bleeding obvious… and perhaps one of the few of us who has the gumption to do it!" - **Rachel Collis, songwriter, performer.**

"The first time I heard Jason speak he spoke truth, truth that I might not want to hear. I also heard weirdness and rabbit holes and language that I could not let my mother hear. These poems remind me of those times - of curiosity, revelation, compassion and downright surprise – enjoy!" - **Michelle.**

"The epitome of rhyme and reason, with a generous side of humour… capable of making you feel a childish giddiness - even with tough adult subjects you wouldn't typically think you could… the balance between shamelessness and tenderness takes a little while to believe. Yet the laugh or catharsis (or both) that it provides is instant… the collection feels holistic and demonstrates textual integrity as each poem flows into the next and has a conversation with the other about climate change, Christianity, racism, sex and more. *I'm not a Racist* is a load of shit, but as this book will soon teach you - what a relief that is!" - **Defne, WestSide Poetry Slam.**

"Igniting flashes of wakefulness through a lively, poetic commentary on the subtleties of life… courageously open, deliciously challenging and crafted from a vast space of deep compassion." - **Lisa Brown, psychologist & environmental activist.**

Contents

Acknowledging Country 10
Introduction 11
Sex is fun, but that's not why we do it 14
Never be the same again 22
Fucking is Fun, that's why we do it 25
Evolution explains a lot 31
Complaint 34
Poo Baby 39
Labels (poo face) 43
Secret Sacred Stories 48
C-Word 53
FJ (euthanasia) 58
Racist butt 60
Interlude 65
Democracy 66
Face Pillow 69
Inga Muscio 73
Sex is fun, so why don't we do it? 77
Gay Carbon 81
Easter 85
Christmas- pash or cash 89

A.S. is	92
Finn Finishes	97
Make us gay	98
Poo- a love story	100
Lick you where? Struggles with Christian discipleship	103
Blokes birthed the Bible:	108
The Chimp's Koran	112
The Bible series	117
How to read the bible	132
Won't come again	135
Preacher poet	137
Coal in Labor-	139
Go kid free	141
Airport hypocrite	145
Bullet for you	148
Baby poem	149
Shut up, poem	151
ScoMo says it's fine	152
Eat me tree	154
FJ and Face Pillow Qualifier	156
Why fuck the horse?	159
A lover in action	161
Acknowledging Country a bit	163

Acknowledging Country

Most of these poems here,
gestated on the land of the Gumbaynggirr

Who've walked this land for 15 million dawns
long before Jesus, or Abraham were born

The elders I've met
are all worth respect
and to the rest I give it as well.

To exist after centuries of hell,
coming through with grace and rage and resilience
You humble us.
You're bloody brilliant!

> If you are looking for ways to make direct restitution for benefitting from a couple of centuries of invasion and colonisation, your local Land Council will probably gladly collect it for you, or you could check out
>
> https://paytherent.net.au/about-us/

Introduction

My dinner didn't know whether to spurt out my bottom, or explode out of my mouth, as I stood back-stage with twenty other equally terrified looking people before the 2017 Bellingen Poetry Slam.

I'd never even *seen* a poetry slam before, and I had only ever written three decent poems in my life, all of which I hoped to perform that night. My family was so nervous for me that they stayed home.

Actually, my kids were the main reason I was there. I probably would have kept chickening out forever, except that one night I heard myself telling them to just give some thing or other a go- what did it really matter if it didn't work out?

So, to prove to myself that I wasn't a total hypocrite, there I stood, in black pants, so that if I wet myself nobody would see.

I trembled through the first poem until I got to the bit about sea sponge orgies. People laughed, and I was away!

Here are the ten poems I performed for either the Bellingen, or Australian Poetry Slam, or both, plus another thirty or so which are unperformed, and may stay that way for some time apart from zoom performances, thanks to the pandemic.

There are some videos at jasonjohn.com.au, and I am adding audios in June 2020.

So much work goes into putting on big poetry slams, mostly anonymously. Thanks to everyone involved in the Bellingen Readers Writers Festival, and Word Travel's Australian Poetry Slam.

Aylin and Defne from Westside Poetry Slam let me try out "Racist Butt" and a couple of others. Miriam and Andrew from St Andrews Uniting Church let me perform the poems I didn't get to do for the 2018 APS.

Thanks to my family for showing up to the 2018 Bellingen Slam, after being reassured by my 2017 result. Toni listened to various drafts, and helped make them readable for this book.

A huge thanks to those who offered their kind words at the start of this book, including those who couldn't give their full names given the content of the book. Visit kathyparker.com.au to check out *The Unravelled Heart*; rachelcollis.com for some beautiful musical storytelling; mindfulnesspsychologywellbeing.com to get your head and soul straight; and westwords.com.au/projects/west-side-poetry-slam for some great slammers (online during the virus).

Finally, thanks to Jesus, who not only offered me a career path, but who pops up regularly in the pages that follow.

Sex is fun, but that's not why we do it

This poem has many, many versions. It started during my involvement in the Uniting Church, as our National Assembly responded to the obsession that many conservatives have with homosexuality.
The poem was massively revised during my PhD on evolution and Christianity, and then brutally pruned to get it down to the three minutes required for the Bellingen Poetry Slam.

I even tried to summarise its development in rhyming verse in one version:

Many years ago, my church wrote
'Uniting Faith and Sex'
We got stuck on gays and lesbians
but there was much more in the text
It spoke of right relationships,
in marriage and outside
It spoke of sex as self-transcending,
spiritual, divine.

But it was so very serious,
in a very churchy way
That by the end I felt compelled to write to them
and say –

Sex is fun!
That's why we do it!
Why we do it when you get down to it –
When you get down to it,
when all is said and done
we have sex because sex is fun!

    But then I did more reading:
    for a taxpayer funded PhD,
    and I came to the conclusion that I was wrong,
    you see.
    But before I tell you more about sexual reality
    Let me say a little more
    about the man called me.

    People call me Jason, I've honours in zoology
    I'm also a minister, who has passed theology.
    I studied up on evolution to complete a PhD.
    And I've been a bloke for years, about forty-
    three.

So, I can say, after years of study
and more contemplation.
And a little bit of practice and
my share of consternation, that

Sex *is* fun
but that's not why we do it,
It's only fairly recently that evolution grew it!

And most creatures on Earth
don't even do it at all
They just split in half and then off they crawl
Then homosexuality was the first revolution,
There was only one gender for most of evolution.

Now we have genders, but not just two –
Some species have dozens. Yes, it's true!
Then we have all those whose gender bends
They switch back and forth – it never ends!
Fish girls become boys become women
become men
A cycle repeating again and again.

Even when our gender stays fixed
things can still get a little mixed:
XO, XX, XXX, XXXX, XXXXX
That's just the female sex!

Also XY, XXY, XXXY, XXXXY, XYY
Yes, all kinds exist on the male side.

And if you think that's a little absurd –
The whole thing is reversed in those feathery birds!
I am an XY, a boy bird's a ZZ
So much diversity and we're not finished yet!

Sea sponges can have sex, or do it alone,
Yes, on a whim they can mate, or clone.
Of course, when they have sex
there is no penetration
They just squirt it all out there
and hope for fertilisation.
Sea sponges have orgies
to an unheard-of degree,
Think about *that* when you swim in the sea!

Creatures that *do* penetrate usually have no fun
Just to survive is the main rule of thumb.
Male spiders get eaten unless they are clever,
lots do it once, most bees do it never.
Birds orgasm in the blink of an eye,
Antechinus do it then crawl off to die.

Sex is dangerous, you get dead a lot.
So why didn't life just say, "I'd rather not!"
Well, sex in all its forms has evolved
to help us fight off the common cold.
Well, really to fight off the deadlier types
of viruses, bacteria and even parasites.

We shuffle the deck
when we combine our gametes
It's infections by germs
which sex evolved to defeat!
Sure, we love sex now, we think it's great!
But it started to let us recombinate
All this fuss, all this ingenuity
Just to help each species hang around in perpetuity

Now, whilst drawing morals straight from evolution
Is really pretty dumb
So is quoting Genesis
Like some God given rule of thumb.
Like, some say, "God made Adam and Eve,
not Adam and Steve,"
But we know that's just rubbish

First all sex was same sex
and didn't life flourish!

While I can't vouch for bloke to bloke,
about it many rave,
Or when there's only women –
though for some friends that's the fave.

Often at a wedding
you will hear that God *gave* marriage
I tend to think it's just
a bit of Genesis inspired baggage.
Sure, marriage is great for a stable society.
The very thing Jesus threatened –
he died a man of notoriety.

Yet my wife and I subscribe to it,
using contraception
(well most of the time,
there's been two conceptions)
A lovely little kid, and another just arrived.
The planet's overcrowded yet
I'm glad that they survived.

(Other friends have no kids,
though they have often tried.
It doesn't help when people say,
"it's for God to decide!"
Babies come when a sperm makes it to an egg
Not when God decides it – we do not have to beg.)
Now, sex to get our kids was a highlight bar none,
But we're not having any others,
and sex is still great fun.
It was even more fun after I got the snip
Lucky I'm not Catholic, but a Protestint!

I agree that sex is great for a married woman and a man.
The problem is that some then say
That nobody else can.

But any ethic which ignores the fact that we've evolved
Is an ethic that will leave many problems still unsolved.

Love yourself love your neighbour
Do for them as you'd have done
Jesus' simple little rules
make sex both fair and fun

Sex *is* spiritual, mystical, emotional, relational
Luminous, numinous, even educational.

If you're having sex
I hope you're having fun-
Even if it started to avoid a pathogen!

Now the poem's over. If you want a closer look
at the science & theology
then buy my other book!*

*Which would be out by now, except the first publisher was bought out by a more conservative one just before we signed. I have a great new publisher, and if they don't go broke, the book should be out by September 2020. It's *Christian Sex Today: advice from Moses, Paul, Jesus and Darwin.*

Never be the same again

Our first child never slept unless he was moving. Which shot my plan to do my PhD while he snored under my desk, to pieces. It turned out that my friend, Michaela, who brought all her babies to class where they slept under the desk all day, had freakishly sleepy babies.
So, I did *a lot* of laps of our block.

One of those laps changed everything.

It's the same again, and the same again,
and the same again
As I push you down the street
and I just *beg* you to stay asleep

As we round the corner
and we hit that bloody crack
which jostles you just enough
that when the sun burns full upon your face
it tears you from your sleep.

And you see those flowers
And we have to stop
And I could weep
But we watch, and we watch,
and it feels like bloody hours
"Yes darling, they're beautiful"
And we watch, and we watch, and we…
watch…

As a hangover in a tonne of steel
squeals around the corner
Over the curb, through the dew, through you

Your laugh cut short
My scream never ending
Not through the ambulance, the police
The blood, the mess, the breath test.
The tow-truck that took away the car
that took away your life

Or would have

If not for that quirky little crack
that nudged you just enough
so that when the sun glowed warm upon your face
and invited you to see the flowers
you did.

And sure, it felt like bloody hours
but we watched, and we watched, and we watched
just a little more
So we watched
as the car squealed across the curb
through the dew
straight through the fence
five feet in front of you

And I laughed and I cried
And I danced and I staggered
And I carried you home
And if we do this walk ten thousand times
It will never be the same again.

Fucking is Fun,
that's why we do it

This is part two of *Sex is Fun*. This poem is deliberately called Fucking is Fun. Not to be controversial, but to acknowledge the insight of David Schnarch, in *Passionate Marriage*, that there is a difference between just having sex, or "making love," and really fucking each other. As far as we know it's something only humans achieve, and then only sometimes.

> *"Fucking embodies a lusty, lascivious eagerness for pleasure... a delicious, desirous wantonness. It is the opposite of crudeness; it is sex embellished with erotic virtuosity. There is deliberate intent to arouse (and satisfy) passion. Fucking makes for intense sexual encounters."*
>
> *Schnarch p. 263,409*

The poem also mentions cunts, rather than vaginas or some euphemism like Solomon's "garden". This isn't just because cunt rhymed, but because I'm persuaded that it's good to talk about female anatomy apart from its relation to male anatomy. "Vagina" comes from the word for sheath. It's the holder for the male "sword."

Cunt has a contested etymology, and not all women are convinced that it could or should be reclaimed, but it's telling that what was once a straightforward word for women's genitals is probably now the most offensive of all English words.
So, with Inga Muscio (see the poem below) and others, I chose to use cunt in its original, straightforward meaning at the poetry slam. I stuck with it even when I realised that the event, which had always been 18+, was no longer.

As one of my kid's friends commented at school the next day, "Well, I did not expect your dad to say *that!*"
And, admittedly, since most people there knew I was a Uniting Church minister, I wanted to mess with their expectations ;-)

Fucking is fun, that's why we do it,
why we do it when you get down to it.
When you get down to it,
when all's said and done,
we like fucking, fucking is fun.

Most creatures don't fuck they just have sex.
Reproduction is the goal for the rest.
Get it in, get it out, get away,
and live to have sex another day.
But enough biology, let's talk anthropology.
Chimps may have sex with whomever they can,
but a long drawn out fuck is left to women,
and men.
I much prefer this path of human evolution.
To me it seems a funner solution,
to have lots of sex and make lots of sperm
and add those little touches that make your partner
squirm.
Intention, connection, passion, attention
panting, pulling, grinding, looking
into each other's eyes,
or at the sweat running down a back
Putting some imagination into my invagination
Doing and being done. Having a lot of fun.

But after the agricultural revolution
men came up with an odd solution.
To make sure that their property
passed just to their own runts,
they somehow got control of all the women's cunts.

It took ingenuity, violence,
and a millennium or more
to sell the world the story
of the virgin and the whore.
That proper women, even once wed,
are coy, and closed,
and just want their baby to be fed.

That's why vibrators sold so well
(ok, "massage devices")
and Freud saw many women struggling with their
wet thigh vices.

So few men gave them orgasms,
because they focussed on their dick,
instead of the more obvious
excitation of the clit.
Men shoot once, we score then snooze.
"Sorry love – I came first – you lose."
No wonder women seemed to give little truck
to the offer of a fuck.

I'm not sure how often I'd want sex again,
if I never, ever, *ever* came.

But you women aren't frigid, or coy.
That's a patriarchal agricultural ploy.
You can orgasm again and again and again (and
again and again) [sigh].

Now, we're not slaves to our biology
from that nomadic past
but if we understand it,
it can help our marriage last.

Or if lifelong monogamy is not
the way you want to go
by all means try some other style.
Remember this thing though:

Those swinging early humans
lived in tribes egalitarian.
There was shared care of all the kids,
and our world is not back there again.

Perhaps our patriarchal phase is fading,
but it's going to take a while.
Women still bear most of the costs,
and men can run a mile.

Yep, patriarchal problems
confront most of us all,
unless of course your partner
has matching genitals.

Jesus said lots about judgementalism,
and having too much money,
but nothing about dick-free sex
or when there is no cunny

>
> Love yourself love your neighbour…
> Do for them as you'd have done…
>
> Jesus' simple little rules
> make fucking fair, and fun.

Evolution explains a lot

When my first ever slam was over, and I'd come second, I stayed up until dawn from the adrenaline, so I wrote this little ditty. In fact, most poems I write after performing, when I know I won't be able to sleep for hours anyway. Here's some evolutionary psychology for you, giving a behind-the-scenes peak at where all the terror comes from.

Way back in the way back when
explains a lot of the feelings
of women and men

Like walking up to a microphone
For your two minutes of being alone…

There's three hundred sets of predatory eyes
all of them staring at me
and the lizard at the base of my brain
is going fucking insane
All it wants to do is flee
to give this whole thing a miss
or to puff up and yell and hiss,
"You want a piece of this!?"

"That won't work, silly little lizard,"
says the mammal in my head
as it begs me to beg and roll on my back
and pee on the floor and expose my neck.

Then the primate comes to the fore.
'cause all this attention it secretly adores.
And they laughed at my first joke
so, for the cheeky little monkey
it's all hunky
dory

'til the human enters the story
and says "Shit I'm running out of time
'cause I stumbled over that line
so I wont be able to finish the rhyme.
Why do I screw things up all the time?
There's no bloody way I've won
my slam career is over before it's even begun
bloody bloody fuck fuck hell
there goes the ten second warning bell
make something up to get it done
but really, I just want my mum."

The end!
Applause, a whoot or two
9.4, 8.8 and 9.2
Holy crap I nearly won!

Wow, slam poetry's fun!

Complaint

Not surprisingly, someone complained about
Fucking is Fun, to the Bellingen Poetry Slam
organisers, thus delivering me the inspiration
for my first poem the following year…

Someone complained about my poem last year.
Not to me of course,
they bent some poor organiser's ear.

Which is a shame,
because now there's a risk I'll do it again

Where did I go wrong…?
It can't have been the dead baby poem,
because they didn't actually die.
The car missed the pram
and the moral was pretty fine.

It might have been the evolution one,
some people think Darwin was dumb.
Or at least misled, or devil deceived.
People have complained that church money I
receive

When spreading his doctrine of deception
But… probably not at a poetry convention.

It must have been the last poem,
the alliterated one.
Ah! I did criticise patriarchy,
maybe that's where I came undone?

But surely not, here in this town of finger clicking anarchy.
Of torrential rain and blazing sun.
So what could it be.
About that last one?

It can't have been saying C---
Half the people here have those.
Though I suppose,
maybe we're meant to act like nobody knows.

Or if they must be mentioned,
maybe I should use dainty words.
So as not to assault the ears of any who have heard.
I could have said China, or even vagina,
But nah that's an androcentric word:
C---s are more than just a sheath for a male sword

Or Yoni. But he's a male Israeli singer-
Good Lord!
You don't want him between your legs all day.
He'd just get in the way.
And make you walk bow legged
Like you'd been on a horse full of hay

Unless you want yours patted
I won't call it a cat
Our builder called it, "hairy chequebook"
and I still don't understand that.

Maybe the complainant was jealous- and wished
they had one too. I know I surely do.
I could hide my keys and credit card
('til I had to go to the loo)

Actually, I'd have my vagina
a bit higher
Right up in my arm pit, hey.
Then I could get my keys in a flash
Or tickle my-self all day.

Surely it can't have been the c-word
All the euphemisms are worse.
Maybe they just thought I was crap
Or they hate forced rhyming verse.

Well, I'm stumped. I'm at a loss.
Maybe I could just ask them how I made them cross.
They're probably sitting out there, somewhere in front of me.
But what would they look like? Let's see….

By the looks of it
They might have a great big beard, or perhaps they are shaved
Many of you are quite wrinkly.
You're all a little hard to see.

I don't want to caricature them,
I'm sure they're a deep multi-layered mystery
As much as you, or me.
They could be cold and humourless,
but just as likely they are nice, and warm.

Still, I must approach them carefully,
I don't want to push their buttons.
It might be my imagination, but I think that could lead to a screaming confrontation.
Whoever they are.

Hmmm…

Hairy, or shaved. Wrinkly. Hard to see, deep
down nice and warm, a multi layered mystery.
Pushing their button can lead to screaming.
Ah- I just put my finger on it.
I hope it doesn't sound too blunt.
But the person who complained about me
Sounds like a bit of a

Poo Baby

AKA One Strainy day in Bellingen town.

Not everyone has had their baby nearly run
over (*Never be the Same Again*), but I'm willing
to bet many people can identify with this
poem, my second at the Bello Slam in 2018.
It was written for the locals, at a particular
moment in our town's history (the "Street Tree
Conflagration of 2018") but it could be any
400 metre stretch of road, really.

I'm going to have a baby.
A little poo baby.

The contractions keep on coming
stopping me from running
to the toilets down on Church street.

At least I'm still on my feet,
leaning on the post outside the video shop.
Panting, sweating,
wishing the contractions would just stop

I gotta tell you I'm really in a fix,
this feels like a big one
and it's not a Braxton-hicks!

Ok it's passed, time to shuffle meekly down to the
Hammond and Wheatly.
As the setting sun turns the hills golden
over the old Foster site,
I'm holding my sphincter real tight.

"No, I don't want a raffle ticket thanks,"
(My eye is already on the prize)
Just a hundred feet and a left turn,
cross the street then follow the flies.

I make it to the corner,
then another rumble from my tummy.
Yeah, I hate to say it,
I think I'm a bit dilated

I can't do it, I can't.
This baby's going to be born
right here upon the artificial lawn
"Don't push, just breathe. You're doing great."
That's all I heard in class because I got there late.

And I remember Darcy standing here under the
shady trees,
chainsaw in hand, amidst the cheers of a hundred
mad hippies.
If he were here, he'd clear a swathe
through the avocado smashers
and the latte sipping set.
Through the yuppies, through the hippies, through
them all and get
me to that toilet, it's just across the road!

But the chainsaw it was chainless,
and I'm standing here alone.

With one last surge of adrenaline
To avoid all the shame
all the people pointing at me
and sniggering my name
I push every bit of strength
I have into my pelvic floor,
I waddle like a penguin,
and head for the toilet block door.

I stumble past the people playing chess.
White's not doing very well,
they lose another piece
So, there's one place in the world
where Black's ahead at least.

I push on past their contest,
as my butt cheeks slide apart.
I offer White my condolences,
for the game, and for the fart.

Finally, I'm in the loo,
Praise the Lord there was no queue.
Pants half down I slam the door-
and finally I poo.

Then I text the family,
it's the proper thing to do.
Father's doing well. Brown eye.
One pound, twenty-two.

Labels (poo face)

And the scatology just kept coming, though
this time there was a more serious point
eventually! I introduced it at the Bello Slam
by thanking the judges for passing me through
to the third round, so that I could show that I
was neither as vindictive, or shallow, as the
previous two poems had implied.

I wiped my face with my bum today
I didn't mean to, it was an accident, eh.

First, I dried my bum.
Then I dried my face.
Well, a 50/50 chance I guess
that my bum germs upon my face did press.

And the worst thing is I realised last *week* that this
50/50 chance confronted me
every time I rub my cheeks.
And then my cheeks.

Yet I could guarantee
that my face was faecal free
if I would only check the label!

Upper left. Dry bum.
Lower right. Dry face.

But I don't *want* to check the label
There are labels everywhere!

Telling me all the Earth destroying crap
they are putting in our hair
Products, and our food!

I don't want to spend my life in the IGA aisle
Making sure there's not microbead laced dolphin
brains basted in palm oil
in my slave plantation chocolate.

I don't have time for this strife
I have a life. Kids, a wife!
Climate change to address
and gay marriages to bless.
Because if *I* have to check the label
Then *you* have to check the label
And you and you and all of you.
No bloody way!

I want a government with balls,
or the more resilient vagina.

To say, "no more bloody snow peas
coming in from China."
Microbeads- no bloody way!
Not in Australia. Stay away we say!
Not in the world, not on this planet,
ban the bloody things God damn it!

And why do we still have battery eggs!?
I didn't have pubes
when people started to object
To the poultry penitentiaries
and burning off of beaks.
Why is it cheaper to buy mistreated meat?
There should be a fine, or we could just completely
ban it.

No more labels!
Cage egg, barn egg, free range.
Just egg!
It's not that strange
to insist, that we all desist.

Fair trade clothes and coffee?
Screw that.
All trade should be fair,
as a matter of fact.

Weren't we all created equal?
(Or, ok, evolved?)
We don't need more labels.
We need the problem solved!

I guess that sounded angry
and I'm sorry for the spit.
But when confronted by injustice
even Jesus got the shits.
Kicking over tables of the parasitic rich
like Clancy of the Overflow
with his great big whip.

Yelling, "brood of vipers,"
"whitewashed tomb"
"hypocrite!"
That was really rude back then-
it doesn't translate well.
Something like, "You fucking thieving profiteers.
I'll see you all in Hell!"
Admittedly, then they murdered him
or so the gospels tell.
But if you believe in resurrection
you should be brave as well.

Others say it's naïve, unrealistic, dumb
to think that we could ever
get these problems won.

When have humans ever, globally,
got our shit together?

Well how about ozone, suffrage, emancipation
Gay marriage, desegregation,
public health care and education.
Recognition!

The 40-hour week
Apartheid, Berlin Wall
National Parks, Cooperatives
and the vote for all

Gloucester said no to CSG
So did Bentley to the North
The politicians couldn't believe how many people
sallied forth

Together

That's the way we'll be able
to move on from checking each and every label!

Secret Sacred Stories

This is my romance poem. It is also my
invitation and encouragement to people to
share *their* romance poems with others,
especially if they're been pressured not to in
the past.
This is as true a story as it can be, given that it
had to be two minutes long, and mostly
rhyme.

I met this woman
on a sexual harassment committee.
Leading to a dilemma.
I thought she was really pretty,
but did I dare to tell her?
And by me she was quite smitten
but we had *literally* just written
about how inappropriate
it might be to ask people out on a date.

More alarmingly, to me,
she was a singer you see.
In a lesbian feminist band.
So now you understand
my hesitation.

And she knew I was a Christian minister,
not yet legally divorced...

But of course
Sometimes you have to grow up,
and take a chance

So, I asked my friend to ask her friend to ask
her if she could tell her friend to tell my friend to tell me
if she'd like to dance.
She wouldn't.
If you've seen me try, you'd know why.

But she did want a root.
So we got together,
and a few months later I finally let her.

Then we started on a baby,
who we took to our wedding-
Which was to some extent our way of getting
some old church fellas off our back.
You see they were emphatic
that our love, no matter how ecstatic
must be chaste.

My minister was right
When he said "hide the light"
of your love beneath a bushel,
keep it secret, keep it safe
Sure, this may be blessed by the Divine,
but even if it's a pearl
there are plenty of swine.

But.
Even straight white blokes like me
Begin to feel ashamed
if they accept that their love is one which dare not speak its name.

So, I decided to witness,
not beg for forgiveness.

Which sounds brave now,
But I would have quit a dozen times in the years that followed.
Except for every Christian who confronted me with my "disgrace,"
there was another who found us a sign of grace.
Thinking,
"If he's still a minister, maybe I still fit."

And all the while their secret stories
of celebration, hidden 'neath layers of
shame and alienation,
came quietly, circuitously,
into our conversation.
All these tiny sacred stories, feeling so alone
because nobody dares to tell them in church.
For fear of that first stone.

Why am I telling you lot this?
It's not the free catharsis.
I'm hoping that a few of you
after we get up off our arses
and travel home,
will share your stories of celebration
with the church or with the nation.

Google whatiwishisaidinchurch
(that's mine)

Or if you're not inclined,
to tangle with the Divine
there's a bunch of other sites online.

Or you just might
Tell somebody face to face
Tell it as a story of grace, not disgrace.

Go on, take a chance!
Tell someone about that time
you asked the wrong person,
in the wrong place,
at the wrong time,

to dance.

C-Word

The following three poems helped me win the
2019 Bellingen Poetry Slam, and get third
place in the Australian Poetry Slam. I got to
perform at the Sydney Opera House, just like
my kids! Though in a side-room, not the main
stage. C-word was really written for the Bello
Slam, since most people there knew the
history of *Fucking is Fun*, and *Complaint*.
I was lucky enough to also perform it at our
local school strike for climate, where people
went from completely ignoring me (yawn-
another Christian muscling in to a public
forum), to laughing along.

When I was a minister still with a congregation
I caused some consternation,
and even confrontation
When people heard the way I used the C-word

Admittedly,
I used it not just once, this was no accidental slip
I used it a whole bunch of times, I really let it rip.

I thought I'd get away with it,
I'm middle class *and* white
And anyone will tell you that I'm usually polite
But three wise men, anonymously
Said that it was them, or me
That would not take it anymore
So, I was shown, very politely, out the door.

That C-word!
It causes such offense
Which is fair enough, after all, I guess.

Christ was pretty offensive,
he left the temple in a mess.
Kicking over tables and
whipping those who oppress

And what else can you do
when you have to
preach from the bible each week,
and Christ - and his mother - just keep
banging on about injustice, and hypocrisy and greed

And at Christmas time we read about
their life as refugees!
It's not my fault the little child
didn't grow up meek and mild!

Christ wanted us to do stuff, or at least to try
and our leaders to lead us
in justice and compassion
in this world of refugees.
There would be no rotting in detention
and we'd stick to 1.5 degrees-

If we only had a Christian prime minister!

I know, I know, we've already had a few.
We got lots of "thoughts and prayers"
and that's going to continue, if I had to take a punt
With our "pray for rain" prime minister
And his "coal won't hurt you" stunt.

Well neither does a cigarette- 'til you burn it
You smarmy –

And he continues to pray for rain
To Mr Fixit in the sky
But why!?

After WW1 & WW2 (and I could continue)
Wouldn't it be strange
if God got off his arse for climate change?
Came down here and rearranged
the weather
Or sucked all the carbon up to heaven
to make it all better?

Prayers for rain are vanity.
Just stop the fossil fuel subsidy!
Where are the leaders who will *lead* us
not misdirect and deceive us?

But, for every disappointing PM
there's a Miriam, a Byron, a Jacqui, a Jess.
There's one "i" Lisa
and two "ii" Liisa
and most of you, I guess.

There's Toni and Rachel and Pia and Pete
and there's people living up and down *your* street.

You've may have never heard of them.
They may have never heard of you.
Christians Muslims Atheists, Jews
Straights, lgbs and tiqs

All us scraggly little mustard bushes
getting up off our tushes

So, whether your C word is Christ or Compassion
or Climate or Community
or Country

Say your C word loud and clear!
Live your C word
and let's put the fear
of true democracy
right up the jacksy of the fossil fuel plutocracy!

FJ (euthanasia)

mum's got cancer in her brain
which sucks
we didn't kill her though
we love her far too much!

or… maybe not enough
not as much as we loved our dog, i guess
we didn't prolong its distress
when it got cancer in its brain
and just laid there, and pissed itself and shat itself
and stared
no, we put that puppy down
the big green sleep. so quick. so deep.

not mum though
the hospice loves her far too much
and i'm starting to think i don't love her enough

so she pisses herself and shits herself and stares
and they clean her up so that tomorrow she can
piss herself and shit herself and stare…
and piss herself and shit herself and stare…
"not long now," they say
"she hasn't eaten for days,

she'll be dead soon don't you worry
though admittedly it's not happening in a hurry"

then "hey"
they say
"tomorrow's her birthday"
"shall we have a cake?"
i shit you not.
a cake for the zombie in room 22b
who can't bloody eat
and can hardly even see!

that's love
true love
in this hospice it comes ordained from above
"thou shalt not kill"
at least not by quick injection
no only slow starvation
shows love in this, our nation

so she's lying there
because the hospice loves her far too much to kill her
except by making her organs fail
and i don't love her quite enough…
to go to jail

Racist butt

Can a white guy make racism funny? Or more accurately, make a serious point about racism while making people laugh?
Aylin and Defne let me give it a try at what is now the Westside Poetry Slam, in Parramatta. They laughed, so that was a start. It also went fine at the Bellingen Poetry Slam, as I expected because most people knew me and would give me the benefit of the doubt.
But when I realised I was about to give it at the APS national final at the Sydney Opera House, where other poets were doing full on poems about their actual experiences of racism, I was more terrified than before my first ever slam, in fact before my first ever public talk.
I could imagine the silence of 400 people not laughing. But as the panic set in I couldn't make myself remember any of my other poems, so the choice was run away, or run on stage.

And they laughed! The white bums and brown bums and yellow bums too! Whew!

I'm not a racist, but…
I've got a racist butt
Its super white. It's full of shit.
As much as I can I try to ignore it.

It's just kind of there, getting through the day
With a lot of weight to bear
And nothing pleasant to say.
Just the occasional rumble
and letting off a little steam
Nothing *really* worth contesting,
or so it seems to me

But every now and then
my racist bottom goes too far
Out comes a roiling torrent of turds
More offensive than a WhiteLivesMatterToo hashtag
and nearly as absurd

But, I decided to believe that my bottom could be changed.
Maybe if I tried really hard, I might
get my butt to see the light.

So I *showed* my butt the light,
I showed it all round Paramatta
'til a cop said "That's not right!"
"Put that butt away I say- put it away *right now!*"

But how
Can my bottom be changed if it stays in the dark
With no sense of autonomy

With no better job prospects,
than making lots of little jobbies?

How will *my* brown eye see
that other brown eyes aren't the enemy?
That bottoms of all shapes and sizes are being deceived,
because those in control don't want them free-
As they were in days of old.

Days when bottoms of all colours roamed free,
not hidden away.
With the sun on their face
lighting up their bum smiles

As they rippled with muscle from walking for miles.
Hunting antelope, mammoth, reindeer and roo
And from squatting when *they* felt like it
To let out the poo.

Brown bums and white bums and yellow bums too
Their colour dictated by their need to
absorb vitamin D.
You see
that's no basis for discrimination.
How much sun shone in your ancestors' nation
We all bleed red blood.
We all poo brown poo
(unless there's something wrong with you)

So all you bottoms gathered here-
RISE UP!

Give a flatulent cheer!

No longer will the squishy stuff up top control you

Or pit you against the other bottoms
gathered here beside you

They look down on you- they *dare?!*
When all the

                    racist
                homophobic
                misogynistic
                    shit

comes from up there?

You may have the anus,
but the brain is the arsehole!

Take back your sphincter, take back control!

        Say no more, "I'm not a racist, *but…*"

        Say simply, "I'm not a racist butt!"

Interlude

That's it for the poems I have had the opportunity to perform for a live audience, and with the virus around it will probably be a while before I get to do the rest of these- so you're "hearing them here first."

One thing I've found about poetry, is the great catharsis that comes from just saying what I want, without having to pass it through internal and institutional filters first, and without needing any referencing! That is, apart from this one, which I put together for *that* Federal election.

Democracy

Clive Palmer wants more emissions[1]
The COALition too
(Admittedly, not most of them,
but Abbott and his crew[2])
The new boss parades around with lumps[3]
to show how safe coal is
And their policy on their non-policy[4]
is to leave it as it is
Labor has a target now[5]
and just needs to work out how
we'll get it done.
But according to those who know,
they need more ambition
If we are going to use what's fair,
in terms of global emissions[6].

---

[1] https://www.abc.net.au/news/2018-04-26/clive-palmer-seeks-approval-for-monster-mine-near-adani/9698680
[2] https://www.abc.net.au/news/2014-10-13/coal-is-good-for-humanity-pm-tony-abbott-says/5810244
[3] https://www.smh.com.au/politics/federal/ten-moments-that-defined-federal-politics-in-2017-20171221-h08clh.html
[4] https://www.smh.com.au/politics/federal/malcolm-turnbull-removes-all-climate-change-targets-from-energy-policy-in-fresh-bid-to-save-leadership-20180820-p4zyht.html
[5] http://theconversation.com/labor-pledges-45-emissions-cuts-by-2030-but-the-science-says-more-is-needed-51386
[6] http://www.tai.org.au/content/advance-australias-fair-share

One Nation says it's all bullshit,
or that humans aren't to blame[7]
and they'll probably get a seat or two[8]
'cause they've learned to play the game.

The Greens are nearly as divided
as the two big parties are,
but their policies look sensible[9]
if they get the balance of power

Without much stronger targets[10]
the Barrier Reef is finished[11]
And get used to the stench
of a million or more rotting river fish[12]
Some say God gave us dominion[13]...
Well, we're a pretty crappy boss.

---

[7] https://www.qt.com.au/news/pauline-hanson-denies-climate-change-humans/3238920/
[8] https://www.afr.com/news/politics/support-for-one-nation-looms-large-over-lnp-seats-in-next-federal-election-20171127-gztdxw
[9] https://greens.org.au/policies/climate-change-and-energy
[10] https://www.smh.com.au/politics/federal/australia-to-miss-2030-emissions-target-by-massive-margin-20181221-p50no1.html
[11] https://www.theguardian.com/environment/2018/apr/19/great-barrier-reef-30-of-coral-died-in-catastrophic-2016-heatwave
[12] https://www.abc.net.au/news/science/2019-01-16/what-caused-menindee-fish-kill-drought-water-mismanagement/10716080
[13] Pretty much every western theologian before 1970.

Or that we're Co-Creators[14]
but we sure have made a mess.

Whatever metaphor you like[15],
one thing is surely true,

if you're 18 you're a voter
with one clear job to do...

                    VOTE 1 for the Earth this year
                      and for future generations too.

---

[14] Philip J. Hefner, The Human Factor : Evolution, Culture, and Religion, Theology and the Sciences. (Minneapolis, Minn.: Fortress Press, 1993), p. 264.
[15] Explored in John, J, *Biocentric Theology*, PhD Thesis.

Face Pillow

Ok one more gruelling poem, based on incidents
which occurred a couple of years after FJ died.
Then we will be back to some LOLs I promise, or
at least smiles.

Addressing "Cathy"

Hi, Cathy, it's me
No, *me*
I did!
I came to see you yesterday
And the day before!
Every day my love I come knocking on your door
No, it's *me*, Cathy

Addressing the audience

If it happens to me
get me a pillow
quickly

For my face

Don't let me linger in a place
like this
when I can't even remember to piss.
It's no disgrace
it's grace.

Just joking
I'd never encourage you to murder someone.
Even me
when I no longer see

You

That would be illegal to do
and a violation of the Uniting Church Code of
Ethics and Ministerial Practice Section 6.2

So please
don't release me
if I'm imprisoned in this shell,
going around and around in dementia hell
I'll probably be quite happy,
won't even notice that I've shit my nappy

Please, waste your life
visiting the ghost of my life

It's not like there will be anything else for you to do
by then.
Domestic violence? Pffft -a thing of the past.
The climate will be cool at last.
The asylum seekers will be having a blast.

Our new PM, Aunty Barangaroo will have
taxed all corporations retrospectively, too
Once her wife helped her pour oil
on the last of the strife between First and Second
peoples here on this soil
Now called Australia.
No, now called Boodja
(Or maybe south Indonesia)

Yes, make sure I linger as long as I can.
Oblivious
In this utopian
world we will have created

Where the oceans glisten over a rainbow reef
and the forests whisper all day
and sing every dawn
glistening in the morn-
ing dew.

But if
Perchance,
there *is* still work to do
while I slumber all day in my piss and my poo,

then grab me a pillow.

And God bless you!

Inga Muscio

At the 2019 APS NSW final there was a dead-heat for third place, so I needed to use up one of the poems I was saving for the final the next day (FJ). At about one am, a draft of the following poem came to me. I was so keen to perform it, but for reasons that will become clear, I was also pretty apprehensive. By 4pm I'd chickened out, and went with a version of "Never be the same again" instead.

Now that it's finished, I'm daring to hope that I can get to the APS final again, because I just *have* to do this at the Opera House. I kept it short enough to have time for a quick intro:

When I became a Christian in my twenties, I went to a few rallies, and dreamed of speaking to a big crowd, sharing my wisdom in a humorous, humble way. Poetry slams are as close as I'm ever going to get. So, I wrote this explicitly Christian one to indulge my youthful fantasy. If you're not religious, thanks for your indulgence, if you are, feel free to use it in church or bible study.

Jesus…
what a *cunt*

You know.
Strong.
Warm.
Worshipped, adored
much loved
and much abused
both adulated and misused.

You might not agree,
but to me… a bit of a mystery.

Blood.
Life.
Sacrifice
Curly hair?
Maybe lice.

Judas thought he was a pussy.
But Jesus is a *cunt*,

Billions adore him
want to touch and explore him
can't live without him
want to bring joy to him
revolve their life around him
can't go on without him
kneel before him
in Communion touch and taste him
have been born through him
yet struggle to quite put their finger *on* him

While others want to screw him
repress and control him
depilitate and whiten him
domesticate and brighten him.

Make him "nice."
sanitised
blue blooded
meek and mild
no longer passionate and wild.

But they're not fooling me
I've known a cunt or three
and the women who surrounded them
as women surrounded Jesus on that tree.

Wild and free,
transgressing boundaries.
Resilient
Like their cunts they were fucking brilliant!
Jesus was tough
he didn't grow a pair
one little tap on a teste and you collapse in despair.
No,
he grew a vagina

That's why people know him
all the way from here to China

Yep Jesus was a cunt,
and if that offends some men
Then put more cunts in leadership!
Can I hear "AMEN?"

Sex is fun, so why don't we do it?

> About fifteen years after the first draft of *Sex is Fun*, this felt like the final poem in the trilogy.

I see the gleam in her eye.
"Ok kids time for bed! "
"But it's only seven"
You heard what your father said!
They grumble off, we're alone- it's heaven!

So, with great anticipation…

We turn on the TV station!
It's Game of Thrones,
we're a season behind
I know. It's shocking.
But we don't mind
Why have messy, actual sex.
When you can watch it on Netflix?

We *could* have sex every night
and when we do it's great!
But there's one more episode to go
and then it's rather late

It wasn't always like this.
Get rid of the kids and then Netflix
Even when they were right there with us,
we used to have a tryst.

I never imagined I could have sex
with a baby lying there right beside,
but when we were new parents,
we adapted to it fine.

When they're crying and they're screaming
and you're patting their head and rubbing their belly
and you know that if you wait 'til it stops,
you'll never be getting any.

There should be a medal for that,
but then all parents would have won.
Come on- having sex as you pat your baby
can't be the weirdest thing you've done!

You know you're a father
when you can coo at baby and rub their tummy
all whilst giving it to their mummy.
Karma sutra for parents...
reverse breast-feeding mother
rock and ride,
peek a boo bonking
singing by the bed head, head.

It's not like we've stopped now- we're in our forties,
we're not dead.
Although we can't use the couch
we can shake the bed

I mean, my wife is HOT.
I can't believe I get to fuck her.

But more often than not, after we've had our supper
We watch a show or two.
Or three.
Then fall asleep.
I mean, what the hell is wrong with me?
And her?

I don't mean to brag but just between us all.
Before I was vasectomised,
most condoms were too small.

And anyway,
I've moved on from the phallocentric paradigm
I know there's more to it than thrusting
to give her a good time.
What on Earth is wrong with us?
And by us, do I mean you too?

Yeah- actual sex…
… *is* messier than Netflix
… but it's *so much more fun!*

Well this poem's done
I've got somewhere to be and someone to do.
My wife's backstage
I'll seeya in two!

Gay Carbon

I wrote this when the Uniting Church conservatives were hard at work trying to force a recall of our triennial National Assembly. The purpose? To force us to re-consider the decision to allow ministers to preside at marriages of same-sex couples.

It looked like we were about to be forced to spend tens of thousands of dollars reconvening, after having spent 5 of 7 days at our national meeting discussing it. By contrast, we discussed climate change for less than two hours.

The poem was originally about grandkids, but really, it is our children who will be affected. Actually, it is all of us already, especially the poor and non-human creatures. But today's children will have to live with the consequences of our inaction longer.

As some of us argued repeatedly at the time, if you are really worried about families, act on climate change- it's the biggest threat by far!

As you'll see, I recycled some of this into *C-word* and *Easter 2019*.

I guess your kids may
turn out to be gay.
But it's pretty unlikely I have to say.

Thanks to you
and me.
As they explain at the I-P-C-C,
because the skies over this lucky country
are carbonising just a little too quickly
with $CO2$ and $O2C$
you see.

But what can we do
when the guy in charge says "coal won't hurt you!"
And they flipped the last guy
when he said we'd do our bit.
Just a little bit of our bit,
take a tiny economic hit (since he was already rich).
And his successor mocks the greenies who dare bitch
about the carbon, the forests, the soil, the reef
aquifers, oceans, and exported beef,
about pollution and profits
through cancerous growth–

those who offer solutions
through solar and wind
through thrift and equality
and a fair go for all.
Desperate to slow us before we hit the climate
change wall.

SPLAT!

Ah, maybe Al Gore was right-
The differences between hope and despair
Is just a good night
of sleep.
Because last night all I could do was weep.
I just could not see the way
to a future
where our kids grow up gay.

Because our Prime Minister prays

for Mr Fix It in the sky
to sort us out but why
bother

After World War I, and World War 2,
do I need to continue?
Wouldn't it be strange
if God finally got off his arse for climate change?
Came down to rearrange
the weather?
Sucked all the carbon up to heaven?
Made it all better?

Prayers for rain are vanity,
just stop the fossil fuel subsidy!
Our leaders should lead u
but distract and deceive us

So tonight- let's get some sleep
Deep. Deep. Sleep.
So that at the break of day
Our rested hearts may find a way

To build a world where our kids
and their kids
and their kids
and their kids
grow up to be gay.

Easter

The more I do two-minute poems, the less tolerant I am of sermons which are mostly filler. This short rhyming sermon was shared with the very gracious Gleniffer Community church down the road, where I preach once a month. No doubt it will go viral in 2020.

So, it's Easter time again
That's why we gather for prayers and songs
Most of us are Christian
But maybe you got dragged along.

Now there's four versions of this story
which might be a clue
that we need to learn to live with difference.
At least that's what I reckon,
I don't know about you

Five versions if you count Paul,
as Christians tend to do.
We wouldn't be here without him,
all Christians would still be Jews

They differ on what happened
But agree on what to do.

We can call Jesus "Lord, Lord!"
And he won't be that pleased
Unless we've fed and clothed and protected
all the "least of these"
Maybe the ones on Manus Island
Maybe *all* the refugees
Maybe those who will be flooded out
In a world of two degrees
of global warming.
(Climate change if you prefer)
Because the scientists are warning
that we're not even 1/5 of the way
to keeping the climate safe
according to our global commitments as of today.

And our Prime Minister asks us to pray
For rain
To Mr Fixit in the sky
But why?
After World War One and Two,
and I could continue.
Wouldn't it be strange if God intervened
on climate change?

Came down here to fix the weather
Or sucked all the carbon up to heaven
to make it all better?

Prayers for rain are surely vanity
unless they drop the fossil fuel subsidy.

What's this got to do with Easter?
Well that's up to me and you
We can just "believe" in Resurrection
or we can try to live it too.

Whether you believe a physical Jesus
flew up into the clouds
and is somewhere out in space,
or instead in something spiritual
which inspired those who took his place

One thing is clear.

If we claim the Spirit is here
and out there,
and that God loves the world
and that we should too,
then Resurrection isn't just what we believe-
It's what we do.

So, whether you think there were men or angels
or both.
And Jesus is sitting on a cloud
or still wrapped up in his shroud
And he was sent as the Son
or adopted for his obedience
And he only spoke in parables
or gave great Johannine speeches.
If you think they shared a supper,
or he washed their feet, or both
I don't really care.

I want to know if you think the Spirit is here
amongst us, as we gather in his name,
as we hear the call "go forth,"
and together walk his Way
of love for God, ourselves, and others.
Not just sisters and brothers
but enemies too

If you want to leave the world a better place
Then know that I do too.
Let's live Resurrection together
Because there's plenty left to do.

Christmas: pash or cash?

I spent a couple of years as the eco-minister at
Scots Church Adelaide, an elderly, warm and
theologically "progressive" congregation.
I had a great time with my colleague Susan
Wickham, and the Adelaide Ecofaith
Community which I think is still meeting.

But every time I stepped out the door,
especially near Christmas, I was confronted
with the reality that if you took away all the
shops which sold things that people don't
actually need, the place would be almost totally
deserted.

It's an easy poem to write, a challenge to live.
Like most Christmas sermons.
But that's another book: which would make
someone a great Christmas present if I ever get
it finished!

All of the gifts which I never got,
well I guess that I don't miss them much.

Of all of the gifts that I've ever had
the ones I love most are the touch
of a hand at my back and my feet on wet grass,
and my babies' wet kiss on my cheek.

Well I guess that they're right though I hardly
believe it will be Christmas time in a week.

All those signs in the store
that want us to buy more,
telling us that they'll sell us love fast.

Yes they're ten percent off
but they're all made of crap
'cause they don't really want them to last.

Yes those signs in the store
that want me to buy more
To show my great love with some cash.

Call me old fashioned but I'd rather show
My wife that she's loved with a pash.
And my kids with a hug then a game on the rug
'cause in the blink of an eye they'll both go
So I'd rather be round now as much as I can
Than working to pay back what I owe.

So how about this Christmas,
we all stay in the black?
Like the sun weathered skin of that Nazareth chap
who went on about money
and the dangers of wealth
for those trying to nurture
their spiritual health.

Give gifts of love, they won't send you broke
Lots of big hugs (come on, even you blokes!)
To those who want one, offer a kiss
Let's celebrate love, not Capitalist-mis

A.S. is

On the eve of my first attempt at the Australian Poetry Slam, I attended the Sydney semi-final, where people were smiley enough, but largely ignored me, except for the Tasmanians. One of them, Andi Stewart, went on to take second place at the final, and if you haven't seen their work, you really should. AndiStewartPoetry, and on Instagram, galactic_flamingo.

I was really grateful for their kindness when we first met, and for the honesty with which we've been able to connect, in the small windows afforded by the APS since. When I heard that Andi was transitioning from negotiating the tricky paths of Christianity and lesbianism, to the even trickier ones of Christianity and transgenderism, I wrote them this poem in response, and they were happy for me to share it with you.

There's this guy,
this particular guy.
I've known him for a year,
known him a bit.
Well, we spoke once,
and I've seen him strut the stage
But I didn't "see" him.
It's strange.

There's this guy.
He remembers me 'cause I made him cry,
I wasn't being mean I was just being me
and I guess he could see
something of himself in the mirror.

But I didn't see
him yet.
Couldn't see him.

There's this guy
who nobody could see,
even as he made them laugh and weep
with poetic imagery
and challenged them to free
their minds and open their hearts.
And won second place across the whole nation
in the APS competition

There's this guy.
Who didn't see *himself* 'til recently,
because he had not yet come to be
(and no, this isn't some contrived autobiography)

Last night he showed himself to me
(not like *that*, just like
"hey- here I am – this is really me"
"More nearly really me")

And I made him cry again
because I could see him.
Part of him.

And he could see that I could see
and he could understand that I was thinking,
"Hey man."
"Good to see ya."
"Though it's going to be tough to be ya
Sometimes."

There's this guy.
He is Abraham, Israel, Paul and Peter.
He is a rock confronting us in rhyming meter.
He is Andi.
Maybe.

Meaning "courageous" and "valiant."
That sounds about right,
so last night we cried
and I tried to say "I see you"
In a poem,
after I got going.
After we both got going.

To walk the Way in our respective ways
Until we see each other again someday.

Don't fart in this pew
God will know it was you!

Finn Finishes

You had your first exam today
for your HSC.
Only two more weeks to go
and you will finally be free
Free to do lots of mundane crap
and plenty of drudgery
and having to find an income source 'cause
your parents are not wealthy.
Unless you go all feral and
embrace a life of poverty.
That mightn't be so bad for a while,
to live you really don't need much.
There's plenty of food in the forest, the oceans,
the rivers and such.
Tents are cheap, the caravan's free
There's wood for fires to cook your tea.
Then, all grounded and tanned,
you can start to make your mark as a man.

To make the world a better place–
I've had some practise at it now
But even if I could tell you how
I'm out of space

Make us gay

When I was a kid, gay just meant happy. Well not really, but my grandfather kept going on and on about how that's what it meant when *he* was a kid.

Someone warmed the toilet seat for me.
They didn't do it deliberately,
they just happened to be here recently.
Burdened, like me.
Then
[Grunt]
Free

Free to go about their day.
I wonder, did they rise with delight
or was this seat their brief respite
from a day of drudgery, heartache, fear?

Who was the man just sitting here?
And, if here he still did sit
would we get along, or have to admit
that we thought each other's world-views shit?
Our politics, our religion, our sports teams crap.

If I sat here upon his lap
long enough for us to chat
Would it make us gay,
or would he say,
"You bleeding heart greenie Christian!
Please go away"

Poo- a love story

I decided to take a risk and stick with this "poem" even though it doesn't rhyme. Sarah Temporal's workshop planted a tiny seed of heresy in my heart, I guess (sarahtemporal.com)

I love poo.
I do.
I love the loo too.
Once a day, or maybe once a week, my body takes all that weighs me down unnecessarily and –
relief.
Once a day, or maybe once a week, my body takes all that would make me sick if I held onto it and –
relief.

I love poo.
I do.
I need a metaphorical loo.
Imagine.

If once a day, or once a week, our souls took all that
weighs us down unnecessarily and –
relief.
If once a day, or once a week, our souls took all that
would make us sick if we held onto it and –
relief.

We may try to hold
tight
to the sphincter of our souls.

But we know that eventually
it passes beyond our control
and all the spiritual poo
that we've clung onto
escapes in a flurry
like a stinking, eye watering, part digested curry.

Offending those around us.
And though the catharsis could,
feel good,
for a moment,
the pain and the shame of our misdirected
public scatological scattering endures.
How much better if we consciously put our
metaphorical shit down the metaphorical sewer
Or better, into the compost loo

So that what weighs us down and makes us sick
can be transformed.
into beautiful soil,
to nourish a soul.

Lick you where? Struggles with Christian discipleship

In case you haven't come across the name, Bonhoeffer was a German theologian who plotted to assassinate Hitler. He also said enough non-murdery stuff to inspire lots of non-violent Christian activists to quote him a lot.

He said good things, including the quote I use here, but if I could have made it rhyme, I would rather have gone with this quote, in which Lilla Watson sums up the mood of Aboriginal activists in the 1970s, and which also seems pertinent in this poem,

"If you have come to help me, you are wasting your time. If you have come because your liberation is bound up with mine, then let us work together."

It is a very visual poem, so let your mind run free, unless you have Aphantasia, in which case I'll be trying to get a video of it for the website and you can watch that-
jasonjohn.com.au

Baby, I want to lick you... *all*... over...
Where?
Pffft
Yeah, I'll lick you down there.
No, I don't care
About hair.

Oh-
Where?
Oh...
Round the back....
Yeeeeah,
I'm not so sure about that.

I guess, ok, I'll give it a go,
I love you so!

How would you feel, though,
if I started with a bit of a grope,
with some soap,
or some hand gel?
No?
Oh well
...

Or some dilute bleach?
Here in the gap in your peach?
It's just that I heard you pass gas
-No judgment-
But maybe there's still some
caught up in your ass.

[*aside to audience*]
Jesus said,
"Do for others as you'd have them do for you"
But *I* don't want someone licking my poo
hole.

Though through the lens of feminist distrust
of privileging my own perspective
the golden rule begins to rust
and the new objective
is to do for others as *they* want done for them,
which can be hard to fathom.

But then again, it's pretty clear
She wants my tongue in her derriere.
And as Boenhoffer said,
"If the church doesn't live for others then its faith is clearly dead."

Of course, that dead German was riffing off a dead Jew,
Jesus' brother James said, "Those who
consider themselves religious and yet do
not master their tongues deceive themselves."

So come on tongue, don't let me down.
I get *paid* to be a Christian,
so no more messing around!
[*end aside*]

No!
Not stalling my love,
just recalling
why I'm here
at your rear.

[*aside again*]
It's no good
I can't do it!
Not even Jesus' teachings can get me through it

He said,
"There's no greater love than to lay down your life"
for a friend, including your wife.
But I'm not so sure
Anymore,
that a quick death is worse
than going in the back door.

[*end aside, sagging and defeated*]

Sorry love,
Satan's won.
There's no way in hell
I'm licking your bum.

Blokes birthed the Bible

An Introduction to Bible Study

I used the first two lines in a short lecture on anthropocentrism (human centredness) at a *Christ in Creation* conference[16]. When I was asked to give a similar talk a few years later, the rest burbled out.

Blokes birthed the bible
And men mediated its meaning
for many a generation.
Now I'm not insinuating
that this was wrong,
I'm straight out saying it.

But today there's another point I'm making.
It was also written by *Homo sapiens*,
you and me
well, creatures with our ancestry.
Sapiens wrote the scripture,
get the picture?

---

[16] http://unitingearth.org.au

"Maybe not," you say.
Were you there, did you see?
Maybe it was written by a monkey.
Moses or a monkey? How do we choose?
Well, let's look for clues.

Genesis 1. How it all begun,
"Let us make man in our image.
Have dominion! Subdue!"
through
to Genesis 9, where God says to Noah
(but not his wife),
"Now I give it all to you" Woo hoo!

I'm pretty sure humans wrote it, aren't you?

What is a tree hugging Christian to do?
Well, we can dredge up Genesis 2.
The *Adam* from the *Adamah*
Human from the humus.
Created not to own and rule,
But serve and protect.

And yet
"Serve" is usually translated "til"
And that was probably their intention.
The story may be very old
but it was compiled after the invention
of agriculture.
Turning that horrible scrub to garden,
swamp to paddock
filling larders
settling down
claiming titles
erecting fences
"mine."

My land
my animals
my women.

Yep, blokes birthed the bible
And men mediated its meaning
Humans did the writing
And humans do the reading.

But

Because some women worked really hard and long,
with a few male supporters,
the church finally heard their song,
and especially their daughters'.

So perhaps all the other species
can get a look-in too.
not just as pets, or produce,
food or glue.

But as much a part of God's story as me and you.

Of course, they can't work at it "hard and long,"
so it's down to us, their supporters,
to sing their song.

The Chimp's Koran

With apologies to Dr Seuss and poetry lovers everywhere

Regarding the previous poem, I have been "singing their song," sometimes tunefully, for as long as I can remember, inspired by James Herriot, Harry Butler, the Leyland families, and David Attenborough.
I sang it squeakily to some people ravaging our local reef in my late teens. After briefly getting lost in some "big C" Conservative Evangelical Heavenism at my conversion to Christianity in my twenties, I've been privileged to be supported by the church to keep singing this song for the last quarter of a century.
I first put it to rhyme in the nineties in this homage to other creatures, and Dr Seuss.

'Twas a lovely day full of birds and the bees
buzzing around the new Truffula trees.
And I chatted to God as I wended my way
promising we'd all be good stewards, one day.
For we knew our dominion meant compassion,
not bashin'.

Then I wondered and wandered
down Cricklewood lane
where I met a small fellow who may well be insane.

But I promised I'd tell you
what the mangy chap said
so, I'm writing it now while it's still in my head...

He said, "I am the Lorax, I speak for the trees,
I speak for the trees for the trees have no tongues
and I'm asking you sir, at the top of my lungs
just for once use your brain
and undone what you've done!

Your thinking is muddled and terribly wrong,
you think you're more special
than the old Swomee-Swans.
I know you mean well but it won't last for long
unless you can make all your thinking unwrong.

I know that you now know that God's not a man
and that men aren't the centre of God's little plan
God's not on the side of the ruling classes,
and colour's just colour with no special passes.

You suspect the right spots in the biblical books
but there's one little thing you have overly looked
The whole thing is biased: it's thoroughly proven-
It wasn't just written by men, but by humans!

I know you mean well, and you just want to help,
and be a good steward and save the kelp
and live up to the calling
you've had from your birth:
Made in God's image, to care for the Earth.

But you're wrongedy wrong,
wrong
wrong
wrong
wrong
wrong!

You said you're made in God's image, not God!
You think you're a little lower than the angels-
you think you've got first place at God's table.

If only you could read the tortoise Bible,
the chimp's Koran
and the orangutan's Flable.
You would see that everyone thinks that they're best
That they are more special than all of the rest.

Now I can see you look flummoxed,
and angry and sad
but the news that I've newsed you with
is not at all bad!
Remember the thing that you know:
most profound,
that God has more than enough love to go 'round.

Only infants need to be most special, and best,
maturity helps us to value the rest.
If the Brown Bar-ba-loots are as special as you
it doesn't mean that you need to feel blue.
And it doesn't mean that there's nothing to do!

All it means is you're not the top of the heap
Your creaturely neighbours
don't have lives that are cheap.
Save them of course, give them room to grow

Be a good neighbour
don't get carried away
with your plans for expansion-
you'll be compost one day.

Love God,
love your neighbour,
do as you'd have done to you.

That's still the crux, I add nothing new,
But remember, your neighbour isn't just you
(plural)"

The Bible series

I wanted to write a poem for every book of the bible, which teaches people something about what is in the books, as well as highlighting some of the absurdities and horrors. When I started setting some of them to Queen songs, I decided it was time to give it a rest for a bit. Or, maybe I will write a whole Bible musical set to Queen songs.

For now, I offer you the first book of the Hebrew Scriptures, and the four gospels from the Christian biblical witnesses.

If that is just waaaaay too much bible for you, skip to *How to Read the Bible* to get the Reader's Digest version.

Genesis: Noah and the giant peach

I wrote this poem originally for a performance at the Granville Poetry slam, after seeing the new mural in the church hall where we met. Several people were convinced that the mural included at least a few same-sex couples. They were probably right as it turns out, as I discovered when writing this poem.
Whether the same sex attracted animals are an accident, or an act of subversion, we will never know. You never can tell with Baptists.

Pictured are the truly excellent Aylin and Defne, who make everyone feel so welcome at what is now called Westside Poetry Slam.

The perfect God had a perfect plan
To make a perfect world and cap it off with man
(Oh, and woman)
Adam from the *adamah*, earthling from the Earth
Created to serve and protect the Garden
"You had just one job, man!"
Then God made a walking, talking snake
For reasons still unclear
And a tree of death with fruits of delight
Yeah, I know right?
Oh dear.

So, the perfect plan went pretty wrong
No surprises there
A little bit of fratricide
Suddenly cities are popping up world-wide
With bit of polygamy for good measure.
They all lived a bloody long time
And the women were sexy, so the angels thought
So, they made angel-human babies
The Nephilim they called them, nobody knows why
Then the humans all turned totally evil
So, the good God had a good cry

Then he got mad and murdered them all!
And to make it really hurt
He slowly filled the world with water

So that they splashed around then slowly drowned
Instead of giving them embolisms in their head
to make them all very suddenly dead

But Noah lived, and his family, because he was a righteous dude
If by righteous you mean a vindictive alcoholic slaver
Who lay around in the nude.
Yep, the first thing he did was plant a vine
Then brew himself a keg of wine
And pass out drunk with his willy on display
A righteous dude, heh!
When his son saw him and had a giggle
He said, "You snitchy little motherfucker
You can be a slave to both your brothers"

Genesis isn't history
Or even sacred mystery
The one righteous man?
They were taking the piss
Unless you see that you miss
The point

Which brings me to the painting above-
of Noah and the peach
And the same sex entourage emerging
Onto the lovely beach.
Same sex?
Well, perhaps, it's not clear in all cases.
So, let me introduce you to the cast-a
beasts who survived the global disaster
Male and female rhinos both have two horns
So that could be Bruce and Peter, or Sally and Norm

They eat 50 kg of hay a day, 100 for them both
And the flood lasted 40 days, or a year, depending on which verses you quote
So, Noah packed them 4 tonnes of hay, or 36, into his great big boat

The poor elephants were driven out of their mind, by the stink of floating bodies
Bumping up against the ark, all bubbly and rotty
Still, they ate their 190 tonnes of hay, making 100 tonnes of poo
All African elephants have tusks, so they could be hetero too

The gorillas are suss
I'm pretty sure that's Bernard, and Gus.
Note the prominent cranial ridge, and they are both
as big as a fridge

The horses, who can tell
They wouldn't hang around to say
With two enormous hetero lions
Right behind them, hey?

Then there's the lesbian cheetahs
(Neither seems to have a mane
And they are nearly as big as the lions, so neither of
them are babes.)
I guess God intervened with some IVF
Why not?
It worked for Mary (but we're not up to her yet)

The pandas were too grumpy to say
If they are lesbian, or gay
They *had* just walked all the way
From A-
-sia,
carrying several tonnes of bamboo
cause it's so hard to find in the middle east
and it's all they eat, the fussy beasts.

But they are the same size,
So, they must both be girls, or guys

The sheep are tricky to say
Did they have polled herds back in the day?

Whether the parrots are hetero
We really don't know
And same for the dolphins in the water
But really, there ought a
Be a lot more- did they drown?
Hmm.

All that extra water must be salty
Or the dolphin skin would slough off
And these look happy as can be
So, all the fresh-water fish must be on the ark
Until long after the mammals disembark
To give some poor sucker the time
To rid the rivers and lakes of all the brine.

And then there's Noah
The righteous alcoholic vindictive slaver
But lucky for me and you
He could cook a mean BBQ

And it smelt so damn good (see Genesis 8:21)
that God said Ok I won't murder everyone
ever again,
At least by not flood.
Though he went on to demand plenty of blood.

Which is why until recently
On islands like Fiji
They weren't worried about sea level rise
Because of the old missionaries
And this story which promised them protection

But the storms got worse and more people got dead
So, they said, "we have sinned, this is all on our head!"
Then they thought some more
And some of their priests
Said "hang on- our carbon emissions are the least"
Why is God taking it all out on us?
And not those western industrial bastards?

So, they got in their canoes and blocked Newcastle harbour
And they paddled off to Paris and they started shouting louder,

"Hey arseholes- yeah all you carbon sinning scum
It's time to repent, and atone for what you've done
We need a new Ark cause our islands are sinking
So you'd better set aside some nice beachfront
We're thinking!"

And our pollies said, "Sure, you're welcome in Australia
Just get in your boats and sail over here
You can have Sydney harbour
and the national park behind it.

pack your things and we'll make room, you bet!"
As a pair of gender indeterminate pigs flew into the sunset.

Introduction to the Synoptic [17] Gospels

Mark and Matthew and Luke
wrote pretty similar books.
If they tried it today, we'd say, "Hey!
You bloody cheats
do your own work, keep your eyes to your self.
Put some referencing in
and stop misquoting your sources.
Get your stories straight,
what exactly *did* Jesus say about divorces?
Was it the poor, or the poor in spirit?
Did he only speak in parables, or not?
And when he did,
was it on the mount, or on a plain, or both?
Was Simon as stupid as Mark reckons,
or divinely inspired,
when he said that Jesus was God's very Messiah?
At the tomb,
Were there men in white, or angels,
and were there one or two?
When he got up again, did he meet the men
in Jerusalem, Emmaus, or Galilee?
What's that? You say it's a mystery?
Well it bloody wouldn't be if it was up to me!"

---

[17] Meaning- "same looking," ie the gospels of Mark, Matthew and Luke. If you want them to be literal history, they aren't nearly similar enough.

Mark

I like Mark,
None of that nativity crap.
He's so short and adroit,
getting right to the point.
God is here, so do something about it!
Don't keep on talking round and round it.
And I like how dumb the disciples are,
how selfish, how narrow minded.
It makes me think there's hope for me
(Though I don't like being reminded
Of the cross all the time, and having to carry it
I prefer the story where Jesus did all that
and all I have to do is believe
in stuff like the Trinity,
and stop being naughty,
and be glad about what he did for me.)
I like Mark's sense of drama,
His story unfinished, designed to invite
Because if the women just ran away in fright
And kept the whole thing quiet
how come we're still reading it today?
Well, *we* finish the story,
As we follow Jesus' Way,
Because God is here
So, let's do something about it.

Matthew

Good old Matthew.
What a Jew!

His Jesus is the new Moses

A five-act play
Like the five books of the Torah

Jesus is a Revelation!
But less revolution, more reformation.

Do what the Pharisees say
Just don't do what they do

And you will become the ultimate Jew

Luke

Ah Luke, the gentile doctor.
Wrote a gospel for me, and most of you
sure, Jesus was still a Jew,
but in Luke he spends time with everyone else too.

And talks even more about money
and the dangers of wealth for those nurturing
their spiritual health.

Blessed not are Matthew's poor *in spirit*
But just the straight-out poor
And "woe to the rich!" says Jesus, again and again-
To the rich man who's a boss
To the rich man with his barns
To the rich man snubbing Lazarus
Woe to the rich! No heaven for them
(For you? For me?)
Until someone threads the eye of a needle
With a camel, or probably any mammal
For loving money is the root of all evil
But some churches have a *lot* of rich men
So, they do a hell of a lot of contextualisation
Except when it comes time to condemn
Gays, or the leadership of women
"Woe unto them!"

John

John, oh John, you acid tripping freak!
Why the long third person monologues
in which we hear Jesus speak?

And what of love of enemy, and foreigner, and Jew?
You're a touch anti-semitic truth be told,
Though I get it, I do.
I know you've just had a great big fight
And the synagogue turned on you.
But you should watch your language,
There's no knowing what such ranting may do
If a certain German were to quote it.
(I'm thinking Martin Luther, are you?)

I know you just had a schism
and half the congregation buggered off.
We're still having schisms now, I get it,
you just want to blow off
some steam.

But best to write that email then delete
Or you could cause all kinds of cultish conceit.
And undo all that great talk about loving neighbour,
and even foe,
and doing unto others wherever we go.

The other gospels set it up so carefully
But you race off tangentially,
exponentially.

Your ever-caustic
dissing of the gnostic
while you yet seek
to make sense to the Greek
reader
made your Jesus monologues
so bloody oblique
and shrouded in mystery
that alongside our anti-Semitic history
we've barely yet begun
to dump the idea of God as three-in-one.

The *ideas* of God as three-in-one
all these years with God as three-in-one
from just one gospel.
One!
One God in three, for most of our history.

Did you foresee that you'd be the one, wobbly, leg
for the doctrine of the Trinity?

How to read the bible

This is one of my rare poems which doesn't rhyme at all, and has no humour. Like most bible studies.

Find a community of people overrun by another culture, which treats them as inferiors and assumes the right to rule over them.
Read Genesis 1.

Gather around a campfire, tell a few jokes, toast marshmallows and wait for the stars to come out.
Read, or better recite, Genesis 2.

Stay put, have some wine, speculate with wry whimsy about the state of the world.
Read Genesis 3.

In like manner, work your way through the rest of the Old Testament, in whatever locations seem fitting.

Or, if time is pressing, Read Jesus' two-part
summary of the law and the prophets,

"Thou shalt love the Lord thy God with all thy
heart, and with all thy soul, and with all thy mind.

Thou shalt love thy neighbour as thyself."

Return to the star filled sky and the campfire
Read John 1. Or better, recite it.
Find a beautiful, lofty cathedral.
Read the rest of the lofty gospel of John.

Find a road, a hill, a plain, an ocean shore, a field of
weeds and wheat, a field of flowers, some barns, a
wedding and a bunch of feasts. Pay attention.

Find some people living in a land occupied by
foreigners, being ruled through division and
violence, and yet who refuse to acknowledge the
invader's sovereignty
Listen to them read Mark, Matthew and Luke.

Find a dark garden, and a smouldering pile of garbage, and read the Passion stories.

Find a quiet, lonely place where people huddle in fear, and read the resurrection stories.

Find a church (if you can) where there is disagreement, and quarrels, and strife.
Read all the epistles except James.

Find a church (if you can) where there are no quarrels, because people stopped trying to do anything significant a long time ago.
Read James.

Find some people (if you can) who have given up in despair of ever overcoming the massive forces which work to destroy the world and its people for the sake of profit.
Read Revelation.

Won't come again

You can't be too careful with eschatology,
just in case one day "He"
does come back.
Though as a matter of fact
I think the year 2000 was about the last chance
anyone had to say,
"any day"
Or "You never know!"

Yeah. We do.
He isn't going to show.
He didn't come for World War One, or Two.
Or Pol Pot, or deep south slavery.
He isn't coming for you.
Or me.

What to do?

Maybe what he said?
(If you claim to be a disciple)

Buuuut- there's all that stuff about wealth.
And we're a wealthy nation,
the average Christian here
is in no danger of starvation.
Or even a tummy rumble
unless you do the 40-hour famine,
no, much safer to keep banging
on about gay marriage and abortion and the pill
And climate change (just kidding).

Though many Christians will,
admittedly, say global warming is important,
though we rank it number 11
on our list
of things to tell people from which to desist.

Of course, he also said not to be a hypocrite
So, I probably should shut up
It's not like I'm confronted
with an empty cup

Preacher poet

I'm a preacher, and a poet
it's basically the same.
Both have lots of different styles
and most people think they're **all** lame.

Liberal sermons have lots of words
all assiduously compiled,
to lay out a proper argument
for the proper people there.
Who love justice, and being mild,
While the candles glint off our greying hair

Think "poetry reading"
with a glass of red
to people with long attention spans
from the fancy prose they've read.
Nodding wisely with wry grins
As the long, flowing discourse settles in.

Now slam poetry, that's a new thing for me
much more like a Pentecostal rally.

A Polytone. Presentation. Preaching. Performance.
Poetry.

Polypaced: preparing-people-to-please. Be.
        Pleased.   With Me.

Both polymotional and poly*emotional*:
from the highest highs, to the lowest lows
to the earnest whisper because, you know,
both preachers and poets want something from you

The preacher wants the offering filled,
And the poet wants a 9.2.

Coal in Labor–

This is from back in 2019, before the federal
election, when Labor had a half-decent
climate target, though only half decent, and
there was a chance they might win.

At last they have emissions targets
and a real climate policy!
And screw those boffins at the IPCC
Getting all sciency and saying we're only one fifth
of the way to the commitment
we need globally.
Because why should we
go on about the Boomers'
giant emission legacy
on which they built their wealth,
and much of this country?

I don't want a black armband view
of the coal industry.
Sure, our wealth is built on stolen land
and on stolen emissions.

And yeah, if we really want to be fair
we need to be at zero emissions in just ten years
but that causes too many electoral fears.

So, no talk of five times more action:
of making up for all our carbon arrears.
A just transition will never get traction
Who do you think we are- Zacchaeus?

Go kid free

Seth Wynes and Kimberley Nicholas[18] made an assessment of how effective various commonly touted individual actions are at reducing carbon emissions. Their main point was that Government and school education campaigns focus on the least effective changes possible. Shocker.

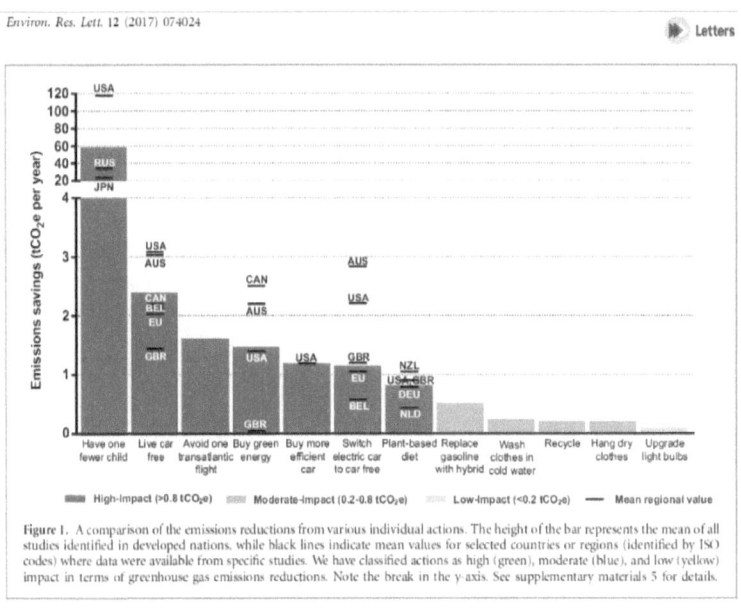

Figure 1. A comparison of the emissions reductions from various individual actions. The height of the bar represents the mean of all studies identified in developed nations, while black lines indicate mean values for selected countries or regions (identified by ISO codes) where data were available from specific studies. We have classified actions as high (green), moderate (blue), and low (yellow) impact in terms of greenhouse gas emissions reductions. Note the break in the y-axis. See supplementary materials 5 for details.

---

[18] "The Climate Mitigation Gap: Education and Government Recommendations Miss the Most Effective Individual Actions." Environmental Research Letters 12 (2017): 074024.

Notice that the first item (having one less child) saves about *sixty* tonnes of CO_2 equivalents a year, and the next item (going car free) saves just *three*.

Why do we continue to congratulate affluent westerners when they say they are expecting a child? Why does the church still offer services of thanksgiving to God for babies? SO many conversations to have, so much difficulty having them!

You changed all your light globes, that's awesome,
and gave the clothes dryer away.
Everything goes in the yellow bin
(everything that should)
You're so good!

You wash your clothes in cold water
And bought a hybrid car (how wealthy you are!)
You went vego (but baulked at vegan)
And you switched to green energy
You stopped flying by plane of course,
Then you went totally car free!
Congratulations, you've done it,
You're climbing the climate friendly ladder
Only one more rung to go:

And it's *thirty* times better
Than when you got ridder
the car
You'll have to keep it in your pants,
Or wear a rubber, or a cup
Take pills or get your tubes tied,
or get the snippity snup!

Yep- if you're a fairly affluent westerner, like me
You need one less kid in your family.
Going car free
Saves three tonnes of CO_2 annually,
but contraception saves *sixty*
That's thirty times more!

As a matter of fact- ya
Can ignore every other rung on the ladder
If you have one less baby.

Or adopt it out to a subsistence farmer in Haiti
Where people live to sixty-three, but they have only
one percent of our GDP
And one percent of our per capita emissions.

So, keep the car, and fly to France
And buy synthetic underpants.
Chuck the paper in the rubbish- you'll be alright
And put incandescent globes back in
so you've got decent light.

Just make sure that twinkle in your eye
Goes dim
or gets shipped out to Haiti
better still, go there yourself
your emissions will drop 99 percent
and your Aussie dollars will buy a lifetime of rent

Airport hypocrite

If you're not willing to send your baby to Haiti, and can't get rid of your car, abandoning flying is the next best thing. The era of the flying holiday is over, and ironically at the time of writing covid-19 has made the culturally impossible, possible. Buuut- when FJ was dying, I flew to see her, and if I could, I'd fly to see nan for her 100th this year.

This airport trip, though, was for *work*. Yeah.

The ensuing self-condemnation spiral, partly countered by the reminder that we can only do so much to resist the consumerist, capitalist system, we have to survive in, reminded me of the letters to the editor in our local paper, which occasionally explode with trolls condemning, for example, those who want to protect our forest from logging, because they aren't also (allegedly) protesting "some other thing," or because they have coffee out with friends.

Skin sickly under fluorescent glow,
while outside the winds blows
ever stronger.

And the longer I'm stuck here the
crazier it seems to fly in *that*.
In fact
to fly at all
with 10,000 scientists issuing yet another warning
about the warming
emergency.

As plane travel increases exponentially,
and ironically
I'm flying to a conference with the ARRCC
(the Australian Religious Response to Climate
Change).
It's so strange
to *fly*, to combat all the CO_2 in the sky

"HYPOCRITE!"

"You latte' sipping, faggot loving, job hating, abbo mating, hand wringing, terrorist supporting, miner destroying, recession bringing, farmer stalking, car driving, online whining, avocado smashing, chardonnay bubble dwelling twat!

How can you say *this* when you do *that?!*
How can you do *that* when you say *this* ?

When you do *that*
when you say *this*
when you do *that*
when you say *this?*
When you say *that*
when you do *this*
when you say *that*
when you do this?"

Ah bliss!

To be someone who yells "HYPOCRITE,"

instead of engaging in this and that and this and that and this.

Bullet for you

Everyone has their Achilles heel. Bullets are mine.

Baby I'd take a bullet for you.
Well,
that's metaphorically true.
If it was real
I don't know how I'd feel
or what I'd do.
I hope I'd stay
But, honestly,
I might run away.

I *really* do like you,
we've been together twenty years.
Had a lot of good times
and raised two great kids

I'd die for *them*, of *course!*
I think.
I could be wrong.
I mean I know my genes will last longer
if they live to procreate
but is that really enough
to ensure that I don't hesitate?

Baby poem

Some babies just never seem to sleep. Others are fine. Which goes a long way towards explaining the difference between the poem I made up for each of our kids in the early days of their births. One of them isn't printable, even in this book, the other is quite sweet.

This little life.
This little spark.
I know one day,
you'll make your mark.
Here on this Earth
your time will come.
In some little way,
your will be done.
This little spark.
This little life.
A time to laugh
a time to cry
a time to rise
a time to fall
be full of grace
throughout it all.
And when at last
your journey ends,
be farewelled
by many friends.
Or even better, by a few
'cause most are gone
ahead of you.

Shut up, poem

For all the wonderful people I've met since I
started doing slam poetry, and that one
insufferable arsehole.

Argh don't get started again!
I don't want to write you
it's three am
and I just want to sleep.

Why must you creep
under the
cozy
comfy
haze
and scratch my brain incessantly?

Ok fine, let me get my phone.
What! No, I'm awake now,
Where do you think you're going?

ScoMo says it's fine

This is *Poo Face* and *C-Word* in a nutshell. I could have titled it "The PM says it's fine", because it was that image of Tony Abbott kneeling at Gina's side[19] which probably first started this poem festering in the back of my brain somewhere. But the second image here[20] finished it. PS, are you allowed to just screenshot someone else's photo and use it on your website? I guess so, since ginarinehart.com.au seemed to, as far as I can tell, though that's just speculation on my part for the sake of comedy and not a legal opinion at all.

---

[19] https://independentaustralia.net/politics/politics-display/gina-rinehart-and-the-ascent-of-madness,4472
[20] https://www.ginarinehart.com.au/garden-party-not-%E2%80%8Ajust-beers-snags-barbecue/

ScoMo says "its fine"
as he turns to the right
and passes Gina the wine.

And I'm a little stingless bee
watching as they dine.
And I'm cursing and I'm swearing
but they don't seem to mind
Because stingless bees are *stingless!*

So, unless

there are a lot of us

Austroplebeia australis

making one hell of a fuss

I fear he will
continue to kneel,
or grovel,
at the feet of his Empruss

Eat me tree

One of my formative spiritual experiences happened walking down a dry riverbed in Monarto, feeling at one with life around me. Part of the great story and family of life about which I was writing for my PhD. I came upon a beautiful, ancient Mallee tree, and rested in its shade for a while.
As I gazed up at the blue sky through the gaps in its canopy, admiring its age and resilience, and hoping many more years for it, I was struck as never before by the fact that the tree didn't give two shits about me in return.
And that that was as it should be.

In fact, if the tree *did* have a consciousness, and could decide my fate, it would be for me to have an aneurysm right there, and slowly rot away to nourish its roots. Its second preference might be that in living, I do something to ensure its long life, rather than just hope for it.
Now that I've written all that, the poem seems kind of short, and I wish I could find a better rhyme than life and survive.

The tree said,

"Why
Don't you just die
right here in my shade?
Then as your body fades
to dust
as well it must,
and you rest from your toil
the worms will turn you into soil
so that I can feast for a whole year.

If you will just stay lying here.

But

if you're determined to continue to be
and to get back to your life,
just make sure you remember me
and help all us trees to survive."

FJ and Face Pillow Qualifier

After finishing *Face Pillow*, and having already
written *FJ*, I thought I'd better write this one too.

Mind as sharp as a tack.
Stretching all the way back
to 1920
or close enough.
I mean, who remembers their birth?

She missed the first big War,
was married during the second one
got stuck with her mother-in-law.
I think Pa had a lot more fun
sailing around in his great big ship
until someone blew it all to shit.

I remember her bossing him around as a kid
"Clem, get them something to drink!"
And the great big bowl of white sugar- divine!
Which I pinched, a pinch at a time.

It wasn't the war that killed Pa
it was his heart, out on the back nine.
On my sixteenth birthday it was
Nan's big grieving time.

She lived with us for a while
and didn't that lead to some sparks.
Adult kids and their parent's, heh!
As I discovered with me and FJ

Then she threw herself into a new place,
a new life.
Painting and walking and eventually Norm
(Though not as his wife)

Then alone again
in another new place.
After nineteen years
she's the only original face

Now it's my nephew's turn
for drinks and sweets.
I'm ten times older than he is,
and half as old as Nan

Her body has slowed down a bit
but she's relatively bloody fit,
and her mind
is as sharp as I want mine to be
if I hit my century.

But… I'd like some way to dull the grief
of losing a husband, a lover, a daughter
without losing all the joy
of what long life has brought her-
grandkids, and great grandkids.
(There won't be great great
Sorry Nan, we all started too late)

So happy birthday Nan!
Well done on not being dead.
If I'm doing as well as you at 100
I'll keep the pillow *under* my head.

Why fuck the horse?

Cara from County Cork used to say,
"Fuck you and the horse you rode in on!"
She probably still does, though she's a vet,
so maybe her insults have moved on.

When she said it
I got a bit cross
what did *it* do?
Why fuck the horse?

But then, because my imagination is so literal,
I went through all the combinations
and decided the horse wouldn't care very much,
in fact, no not at all.
I remembered seeing my old girlfriend's horse,
a stallion "on display,"
and realised that if Cara fucked that horse
She'd be the one waddling away.
And if the horse was a lady
there's not an accessory
in any shop in town
that would even have a chance of
making a mare frown.

And if Cara were instead a man,
perhaps a man called Pat,
and could find a box on which to stand
the mare wouldn't care about that.
Finally, if Pat happened upon a male
and lined up behind its tail,
there would be one hell of a kick
in Pat's dick.

So, fuck the horse if you want to,
just don't expect a big reaction.
And I'm warning you now, if you get one
it'll see you end up in traction.
So much for the horse,
how is "fuck you!" a threat?
Cara was such a beauty
you would have had to be really, *really* gay
not to tap that booty.
And half the women I know, if not more
would become temporarily lesbian for sure
if they raised her ire, and the result
was her famous come on,
I mean, insult.
Most of my poems have morals
But I'm not so sure about this one
Surely you *know* not to fuck a horse
Even if it's what someone rode in on.

A lover in action

Writing gender neutral poetry in English is tedious, I've discovered. But not as tedious as putting up with heteronormativity all day, every day. Hopefully using their and *their* works to differentiate the two people.

They slide their hand inside *their* thigh
Provoking moist reaction
Slipperiness and parted lips
A lover, in action.

They slide their hand inside a glove
Provoking moist reaction
Slippery dishes soon are clean
A lover, in action

They slide their hand in nappy box
Because of some moist action
Sloppy bottom soon is clean
A lover, in action

They clench their hands in rage at *them*
An argument, reaction
Shouting, weeping, silence
A lover, in action

They slide their hand inside *their* thigh
Provoking moist reaction
The kids are out and they're alone
A lover, in action.

They put their hand up to *their* mouth
Pavlovian reaction
Toothless gums chew soggy food
A lover, in action

They lay themself upon *their* grave
Reject all consolation
Moistened eyes and trembling lips
A lover, in action.

Acknowledging Country
a bit

I wanted to write a rhyming acknowledgment of Country to use as MC for the 2020 Bellingen Poetry Slam. The short version is at the start of this book. If you're a Second Australian, I invite you to wrestle with what it means to say we "acknowledge Country" in this longer, more cynical version.

I acknowledge, or maybe concede
That we stand
On Aboriginal land
Never ceded

Which is why I gave my house back…

Well, no, I didn't go as far as that!
I mean "Aboriginal land" in a "spiritual sense"
Not one that has any tangible application
For the property I own in this *our* nation

Like the way I say
"How's it going mate?"
But don't wait for a reply-
Why would I?
No one takes *that* literally.

I mean I'm not *glad* if you're sad
But if you go on about it, you'll make me feel bad
And then I'll probably get mad,
Somewhere behind the smile.
And next time I see you, I'll run a mile.

I mean, I've *acknowledged* that you seem blue
So just shut up about it, why don't you?
It works for mates
And our nation too.

I mean sure,
When I acknowledged that my rent was due
I paid it
When I acknowledged that my dog was hungry
I fed it
When I acknowledged that I was getting fat
I diet-it

But when I acknowledge this is Aboriginal land…

Do I really just mean,
"Hey Uncle, come and welcome us willya?"
But make it quick,
We don't have time for you to spill ya
Guts and spin your yarns

We'll give you two minutes
And two hundred bucks[21]
Keep it light,
We already know it sucks.

> If you are looking for ways to make direct restitution for benefitting from a couple of centuries of invasion and colonisation, your local Land Council will probably gladly collect it for you, or you could check out…
>
> https://paytherent.net.au/about-us/

---

[21] (Or quite possibly not, because you know, money's tight)

Thanks for reading this far.

If all goes according to plan, I'll be putting up audios of all of the poems, to go with the videos I already have of some of them.

Visit http://jasonjohn.com.au to find them, and if you need it enter **racistbutt** as the code.

If it's still covid-19 time when you read this, one of the plusses is that it's now pretty easy to attend poetry performances and readings with people from all over the country, and to have a go yourself! Sarah at sarahtemporal.com was talking about getting together a list.

I'd love to know what you thought, and if I can make your thoughts public, and if you want just your first name, or a link to your own poetry/books- jasonrobertjohn@gmail.com

If you are happy to write a review wherever you got this, I'd love that too.

www.ingramcontent.com/pod-product-compliance
Lightning Source LLC
Chambersburg PA
CBHW032040290426
44110CB00012B/882